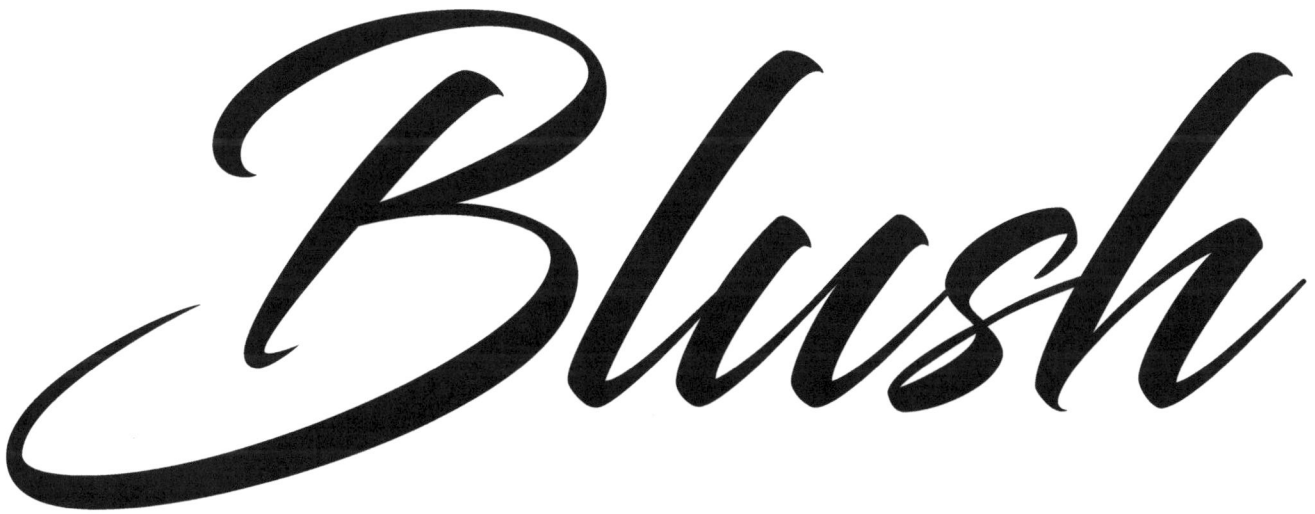

Hot Sexy Lingerie Girls
Models Pictures

By **PHOTO ART LOVER**

Copyright © Blush

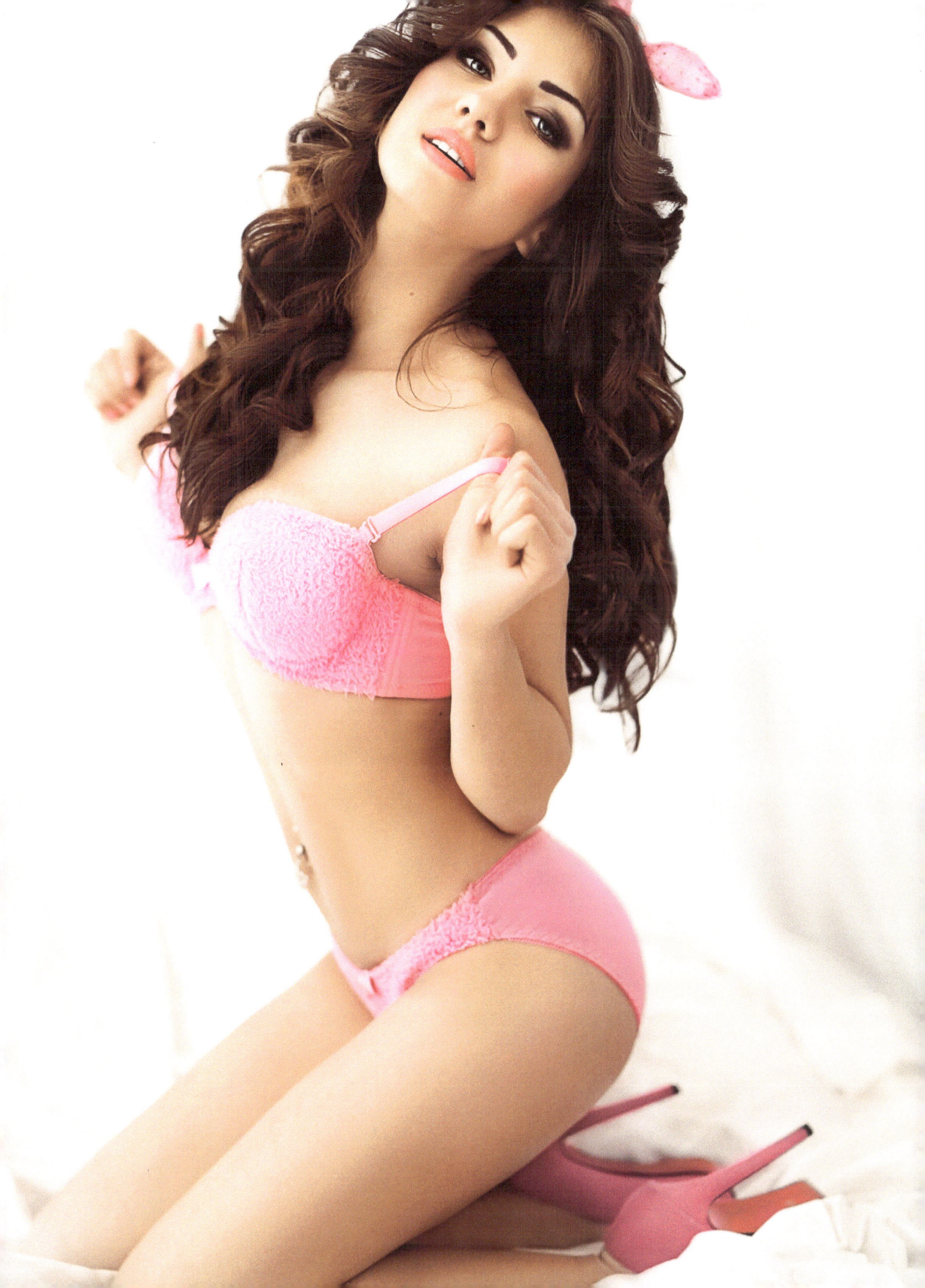

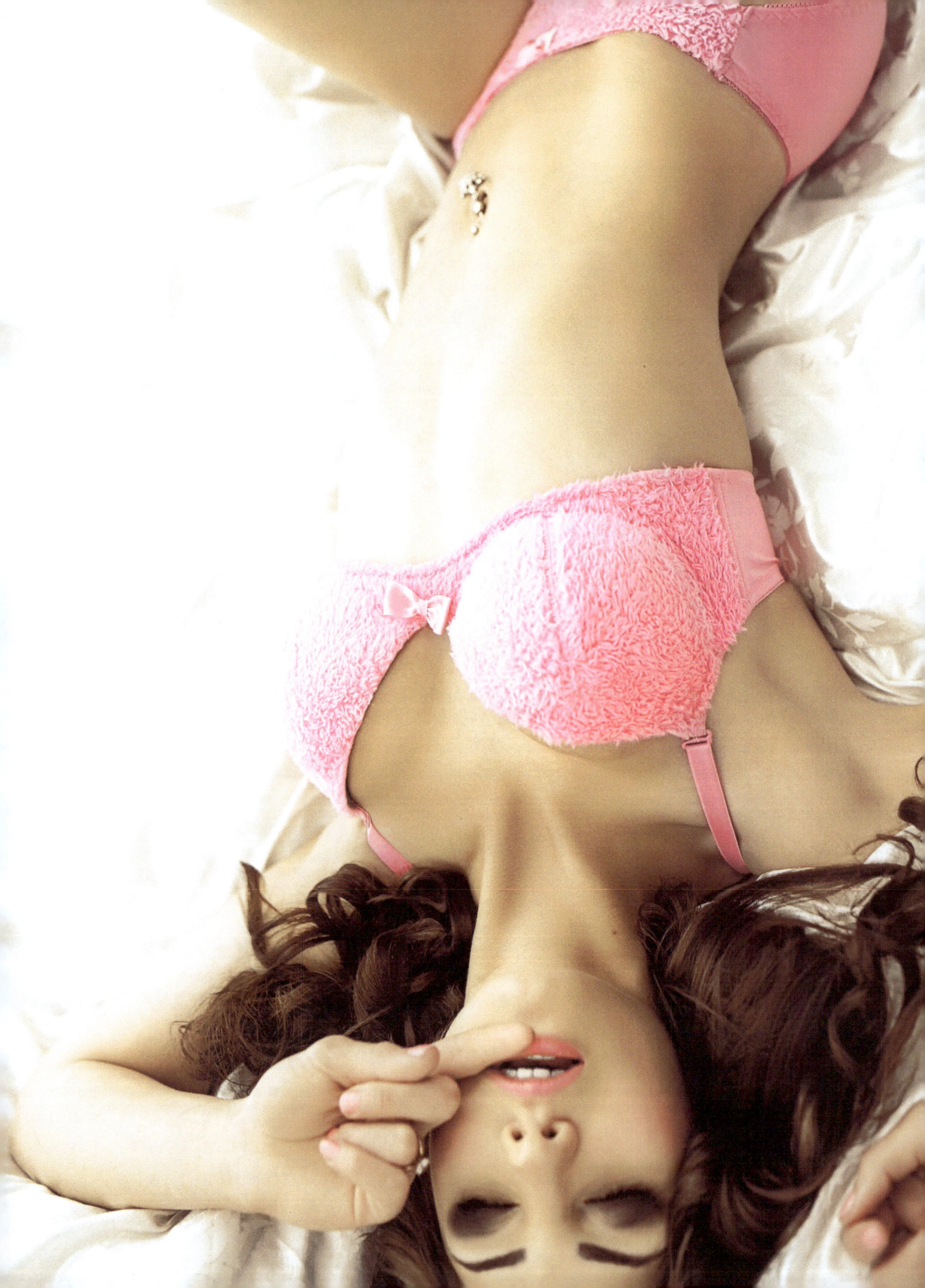

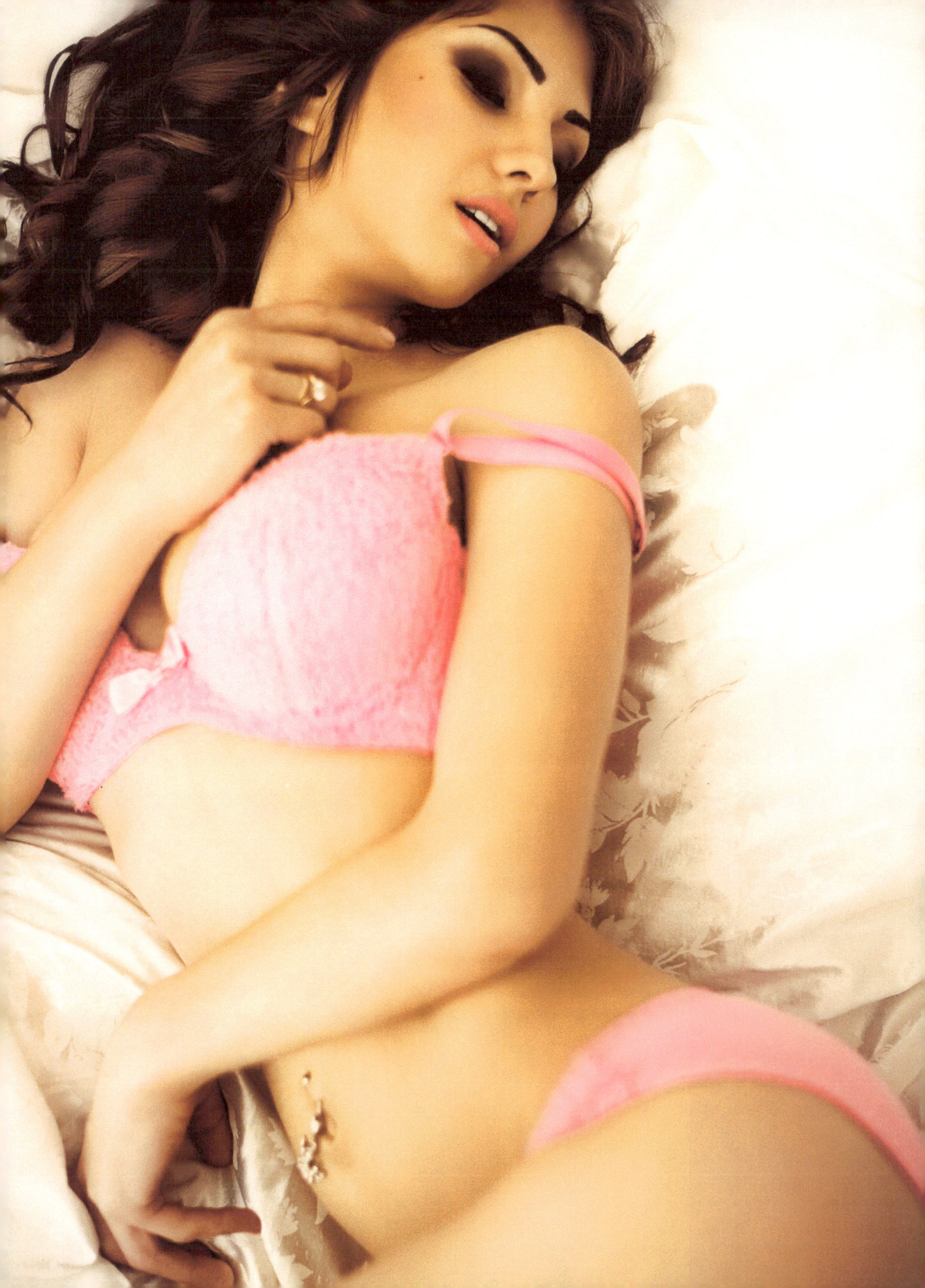

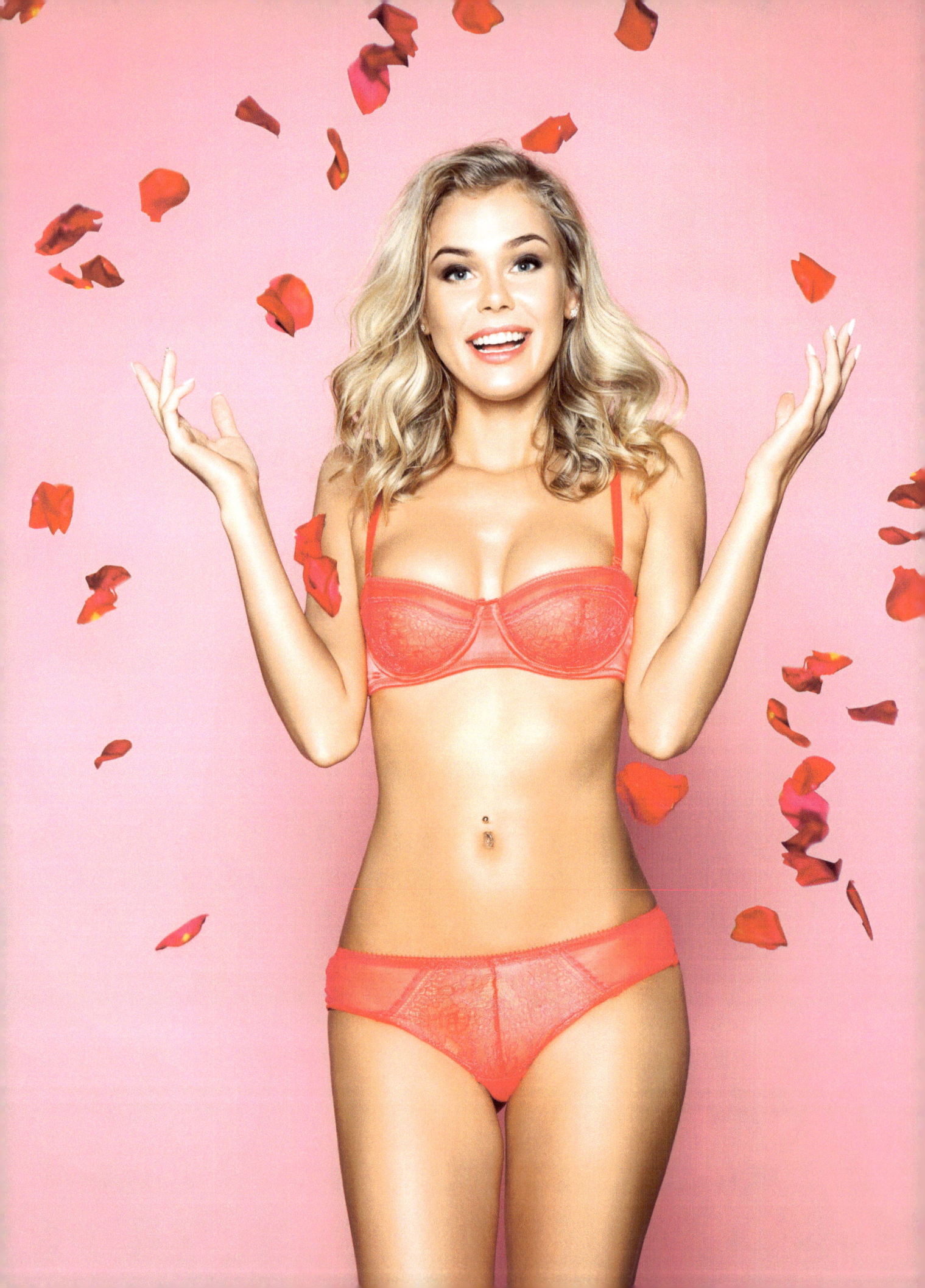

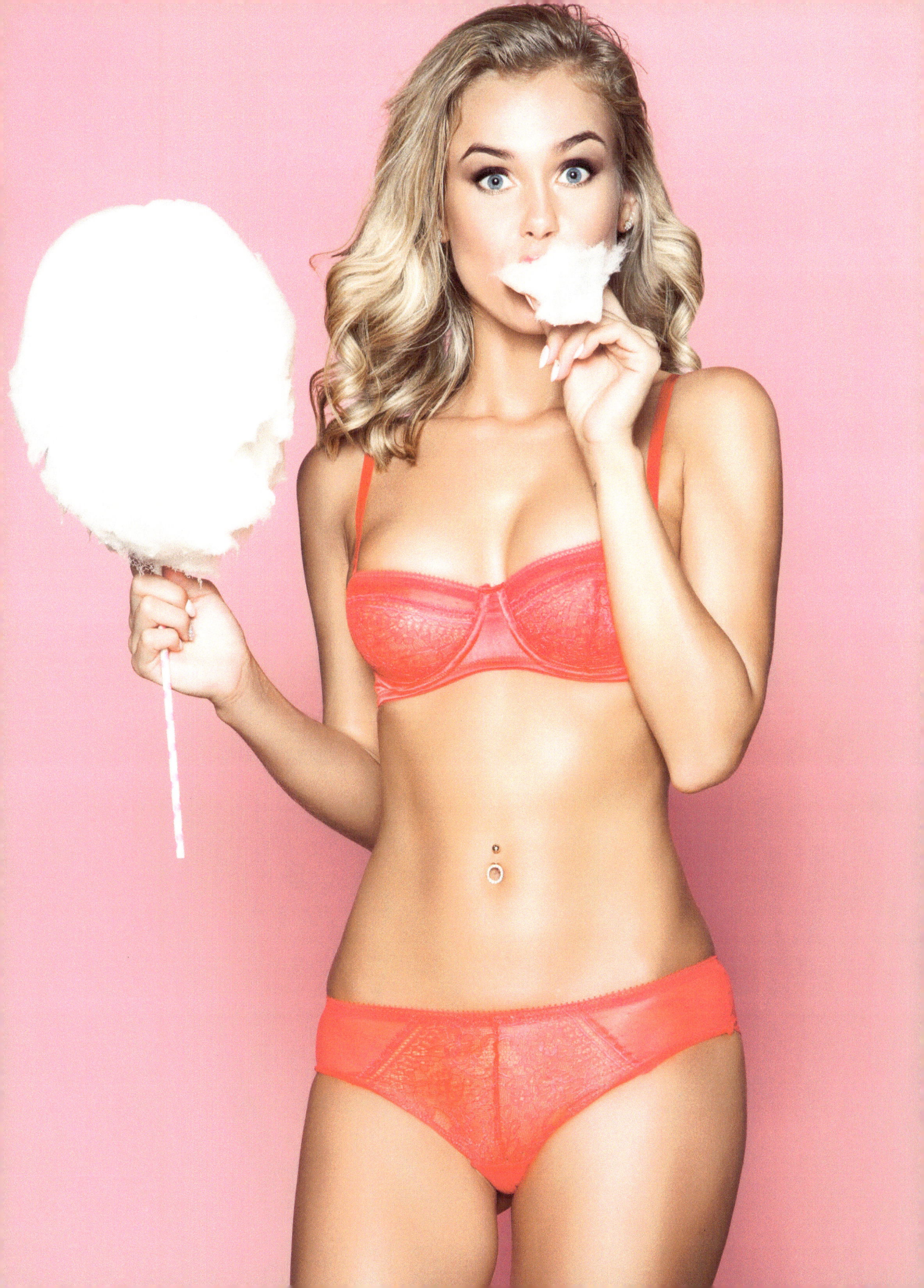

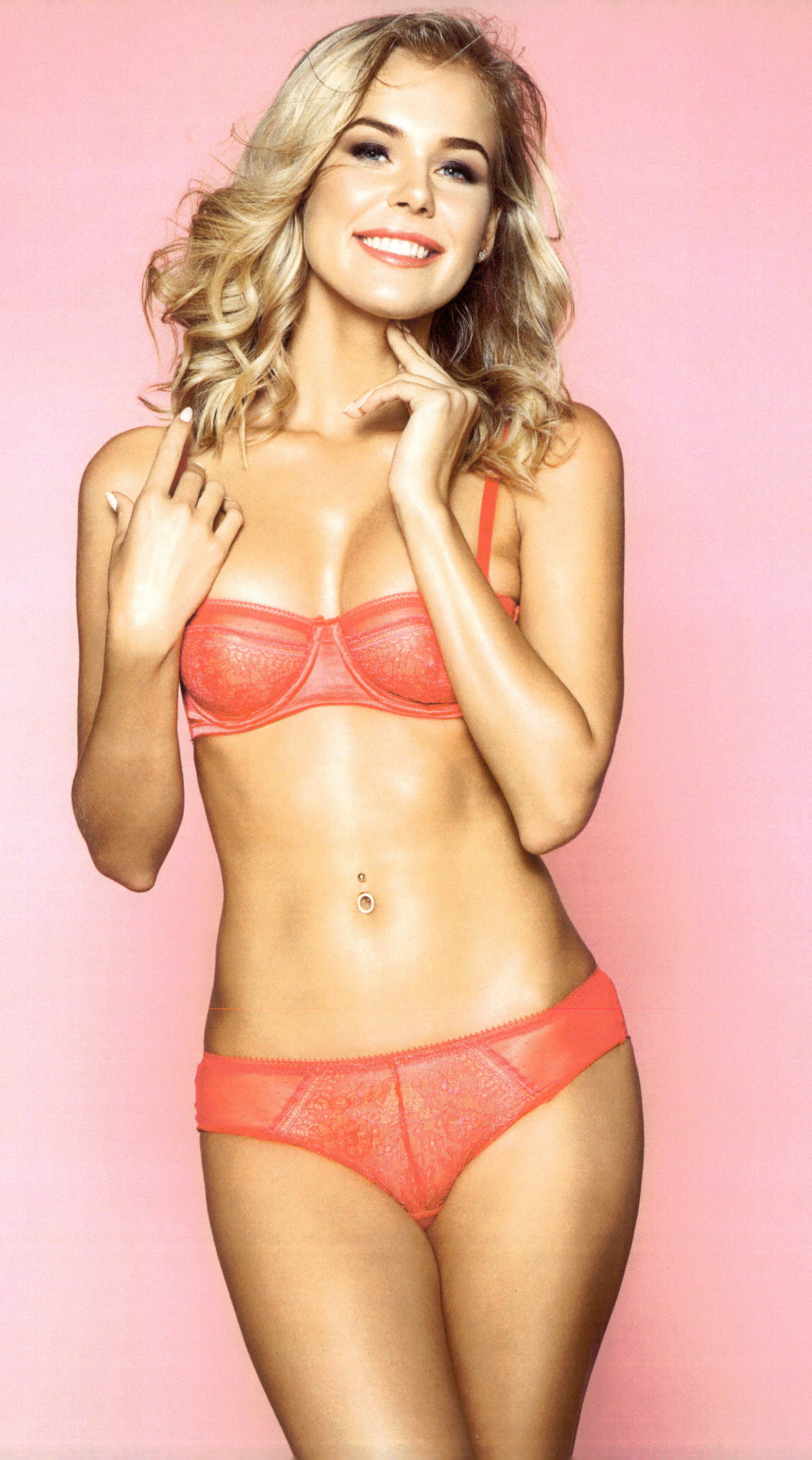

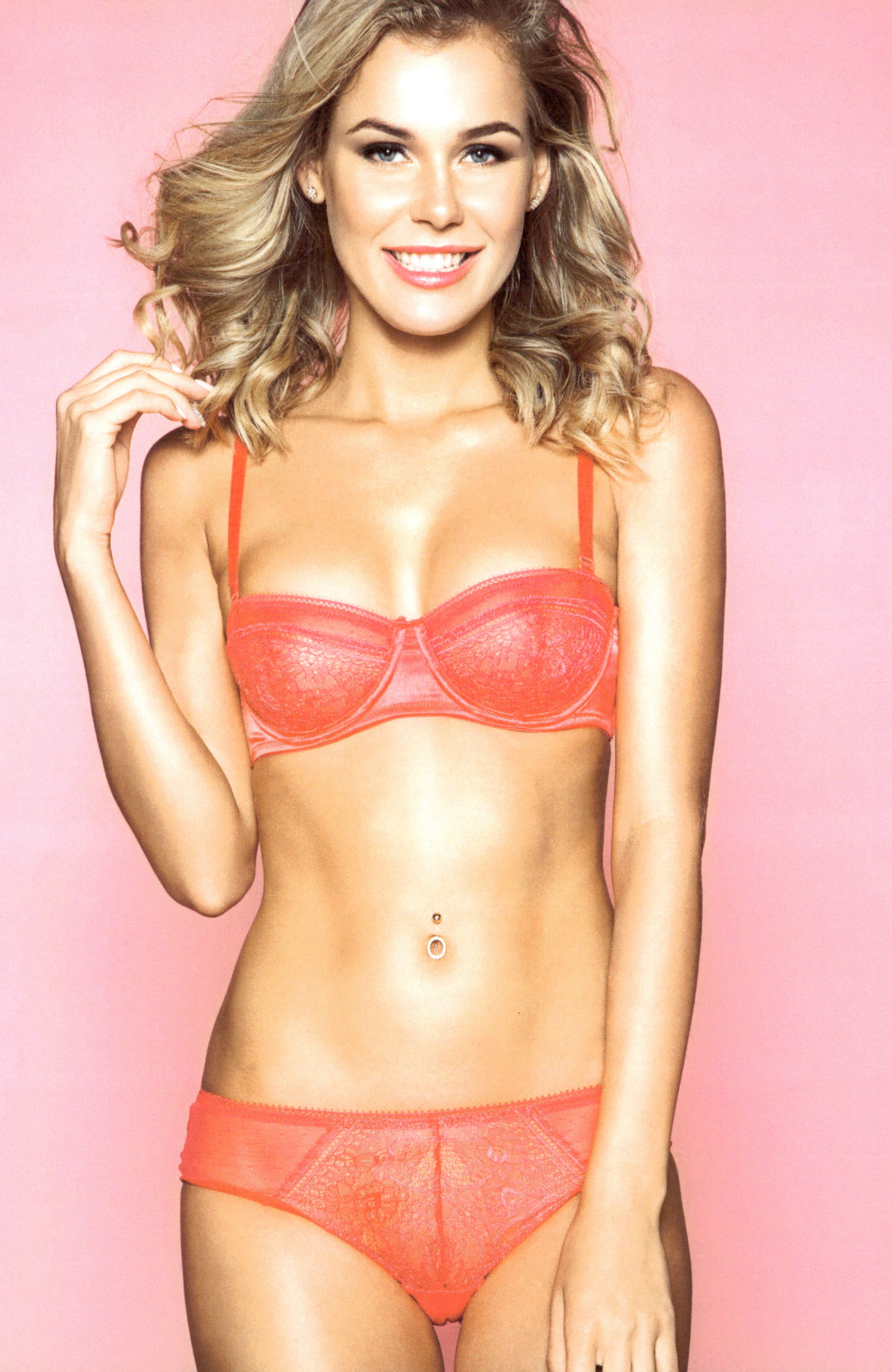

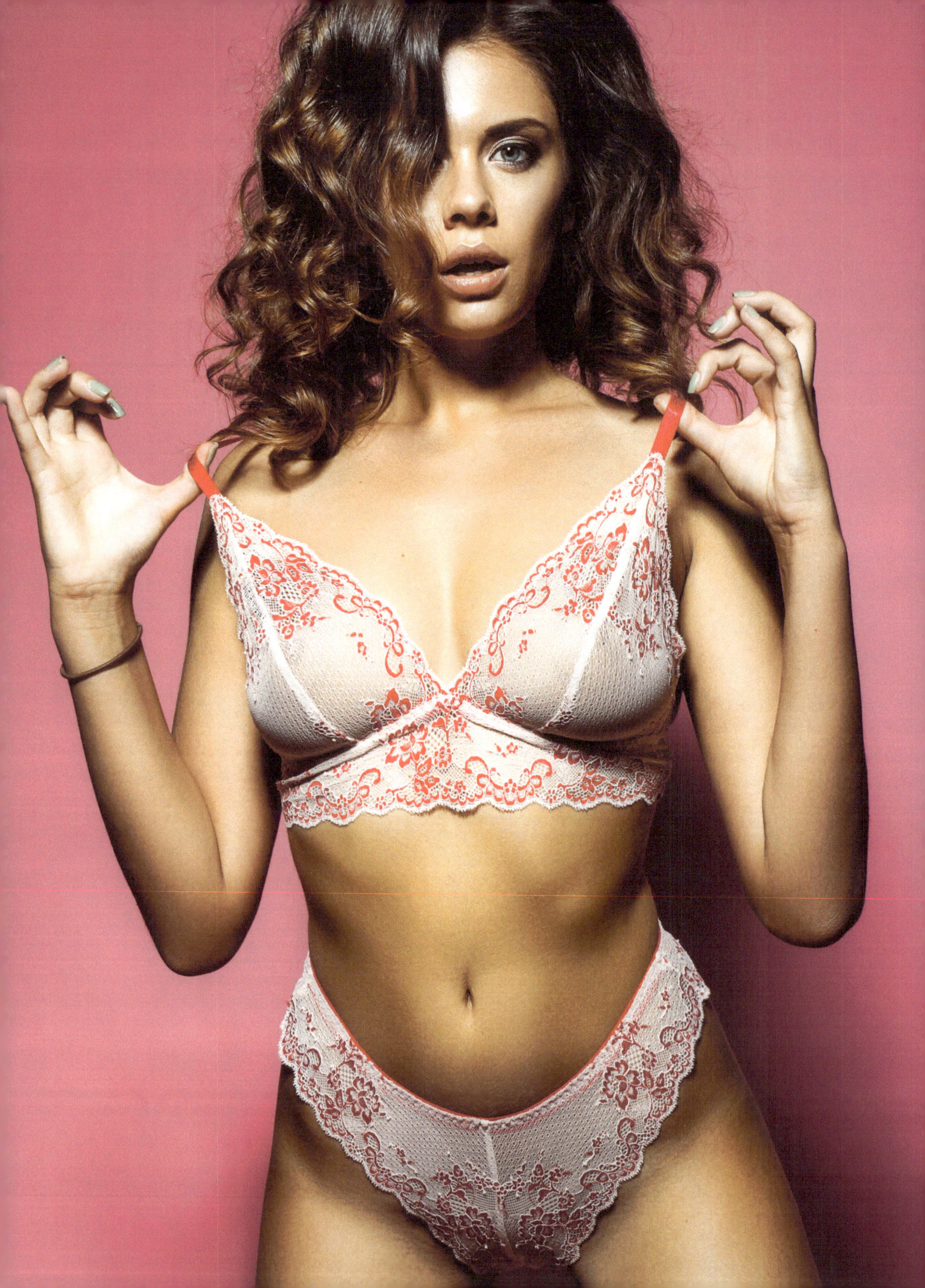

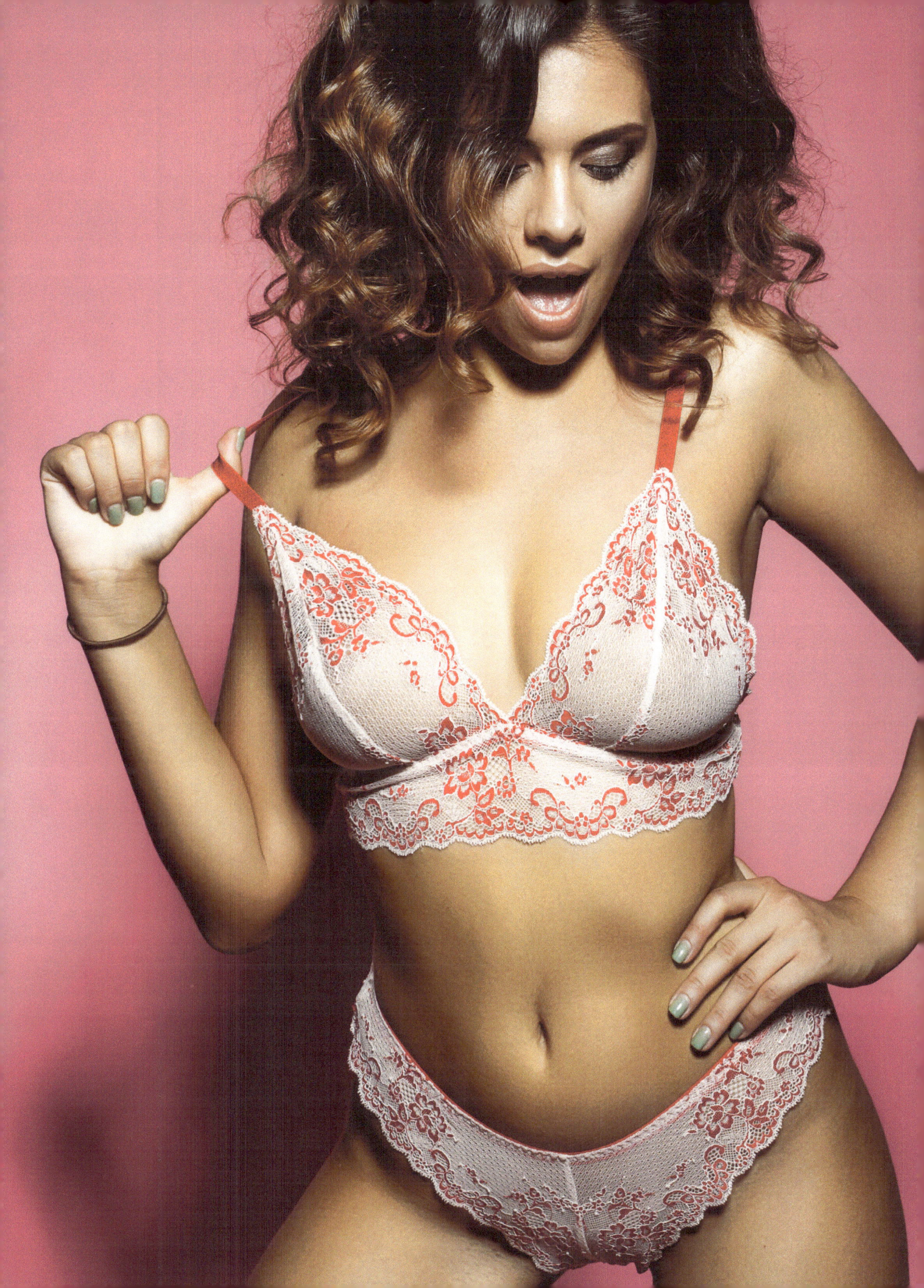

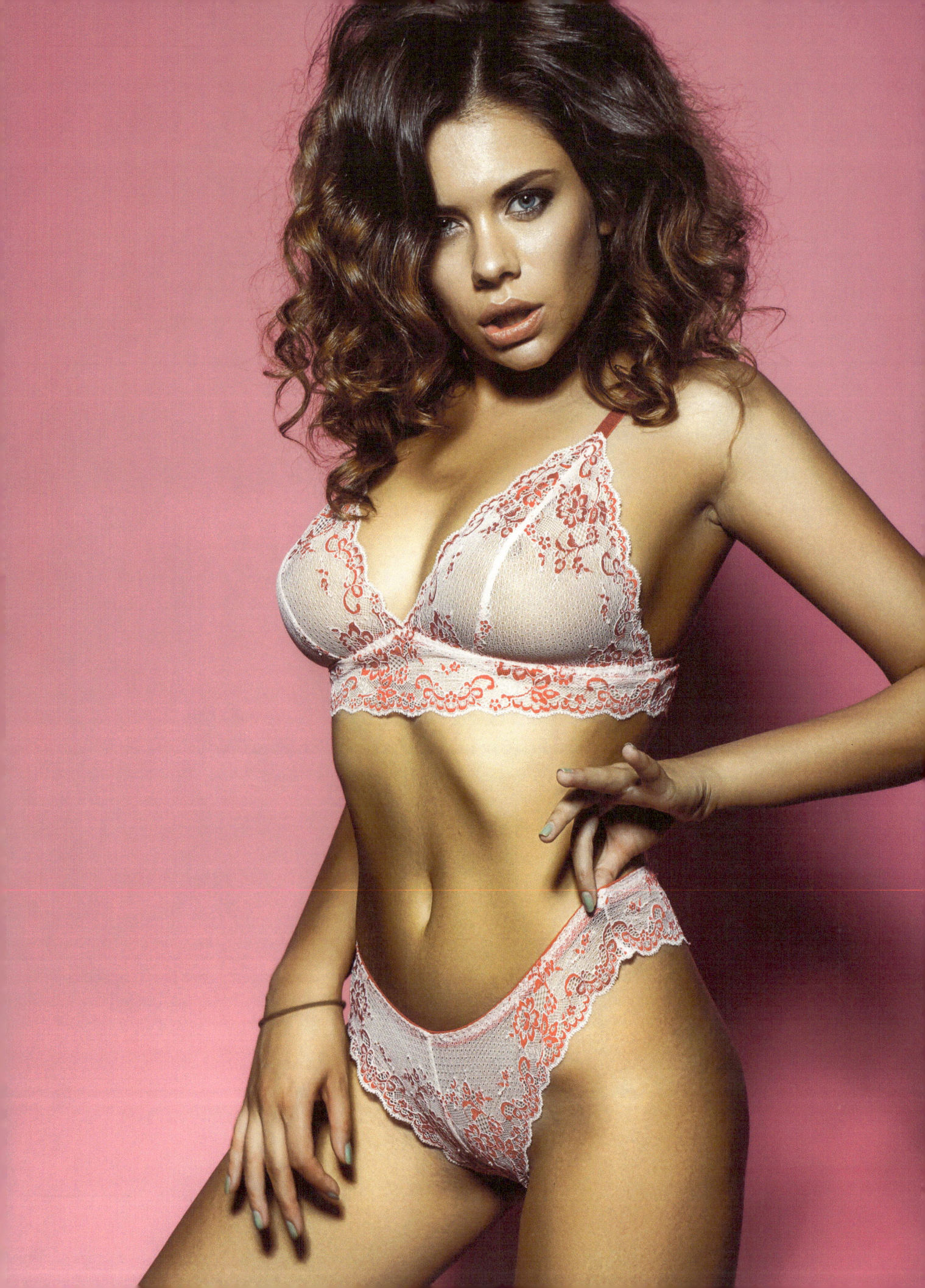

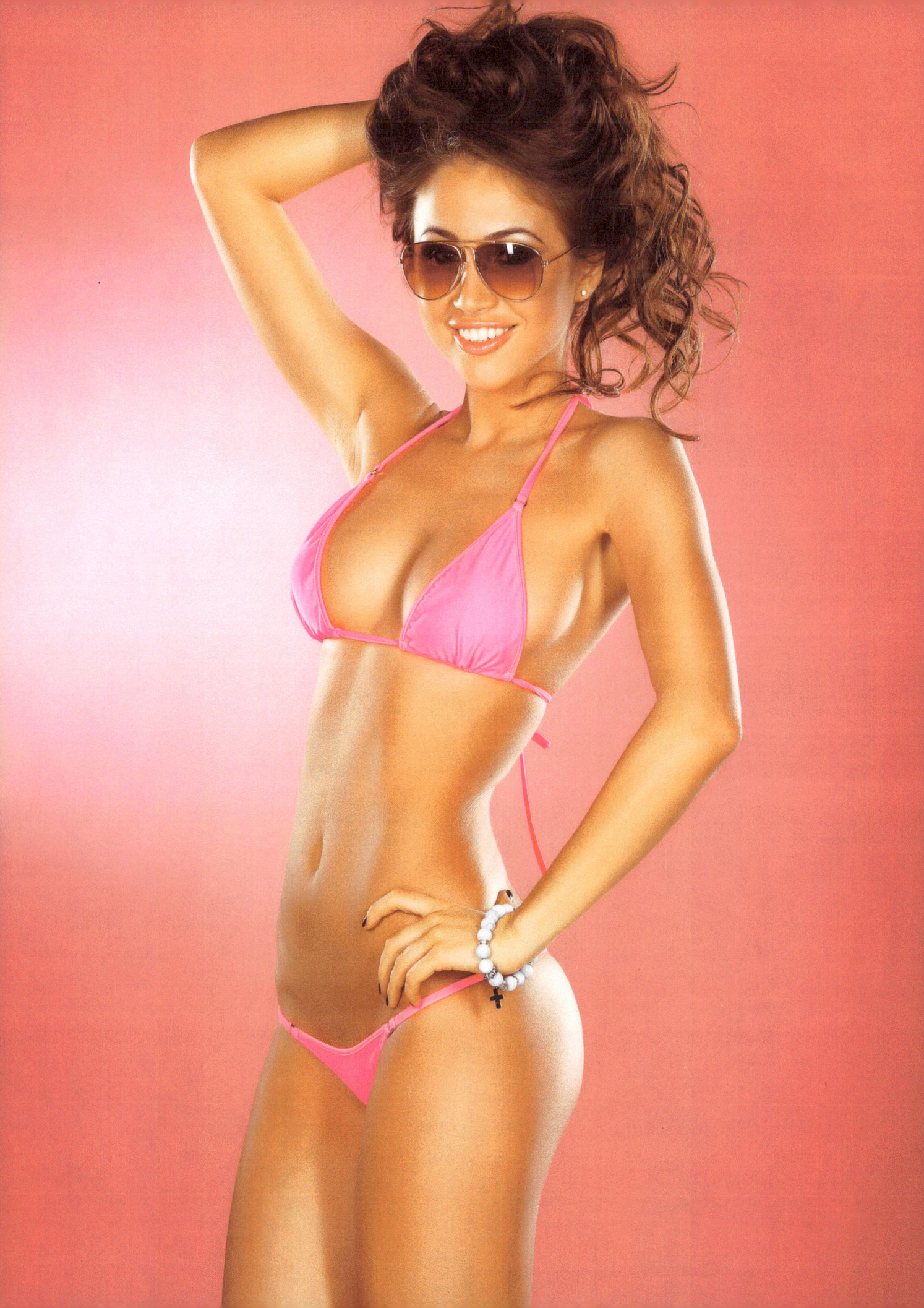

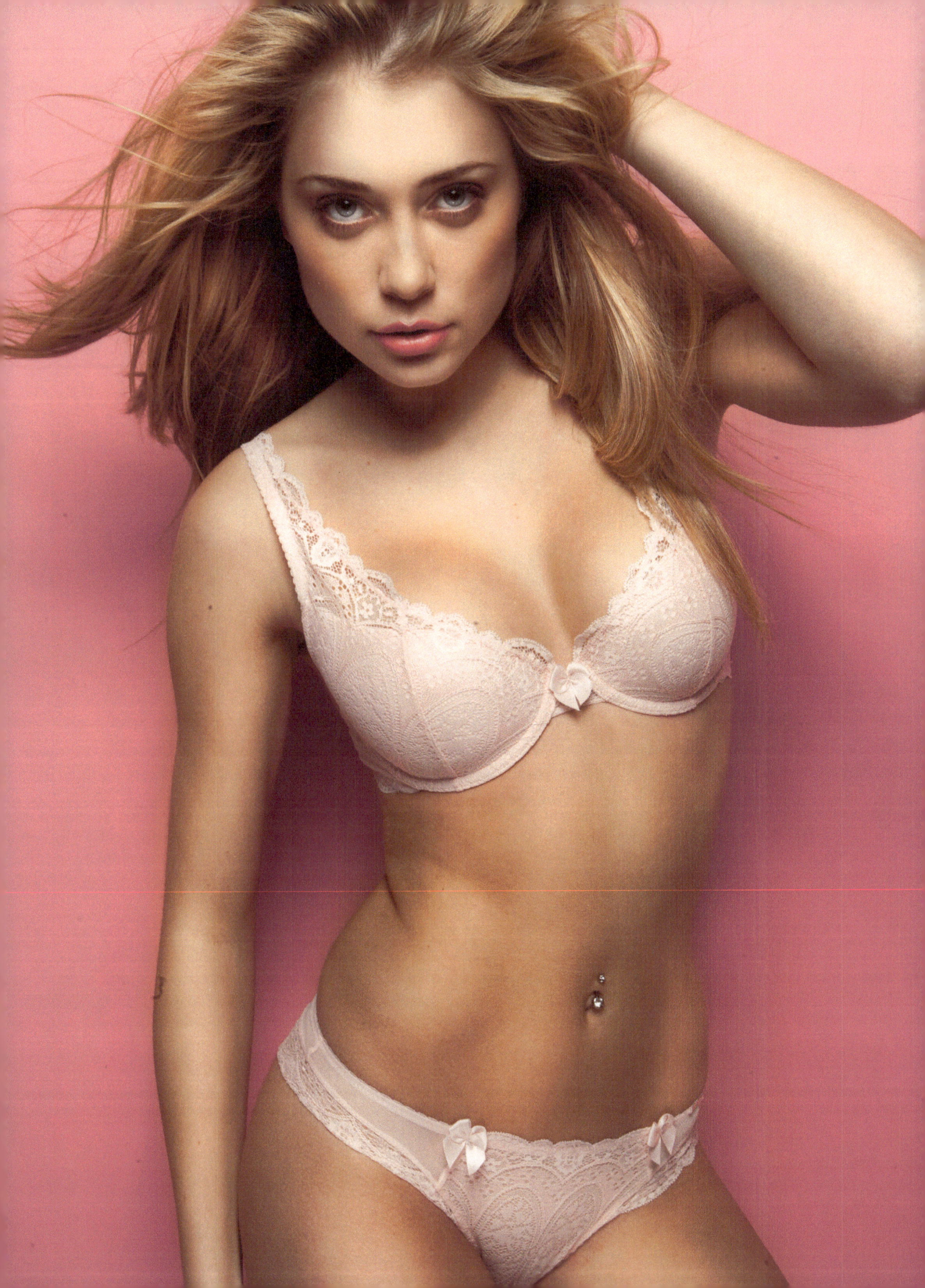

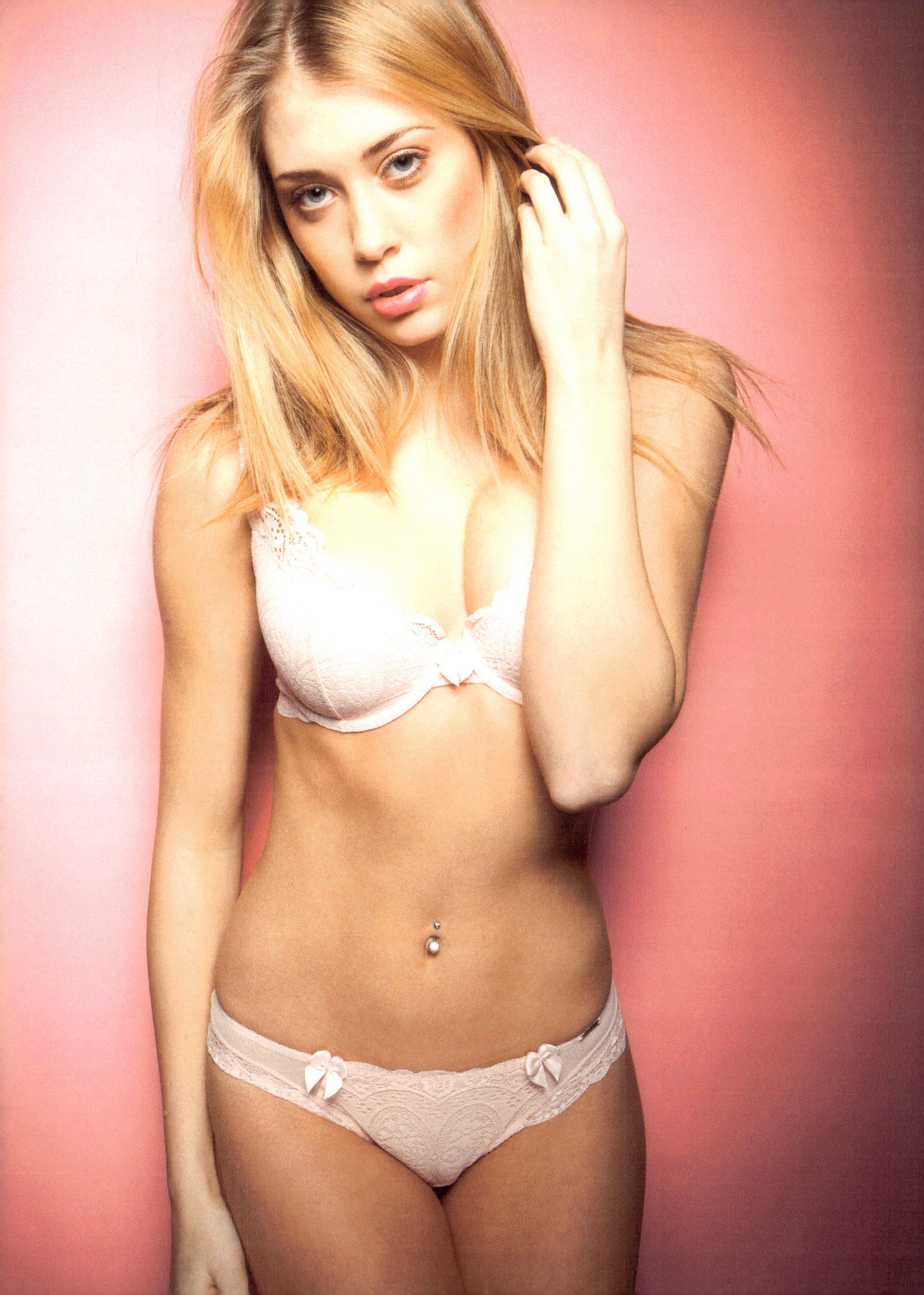

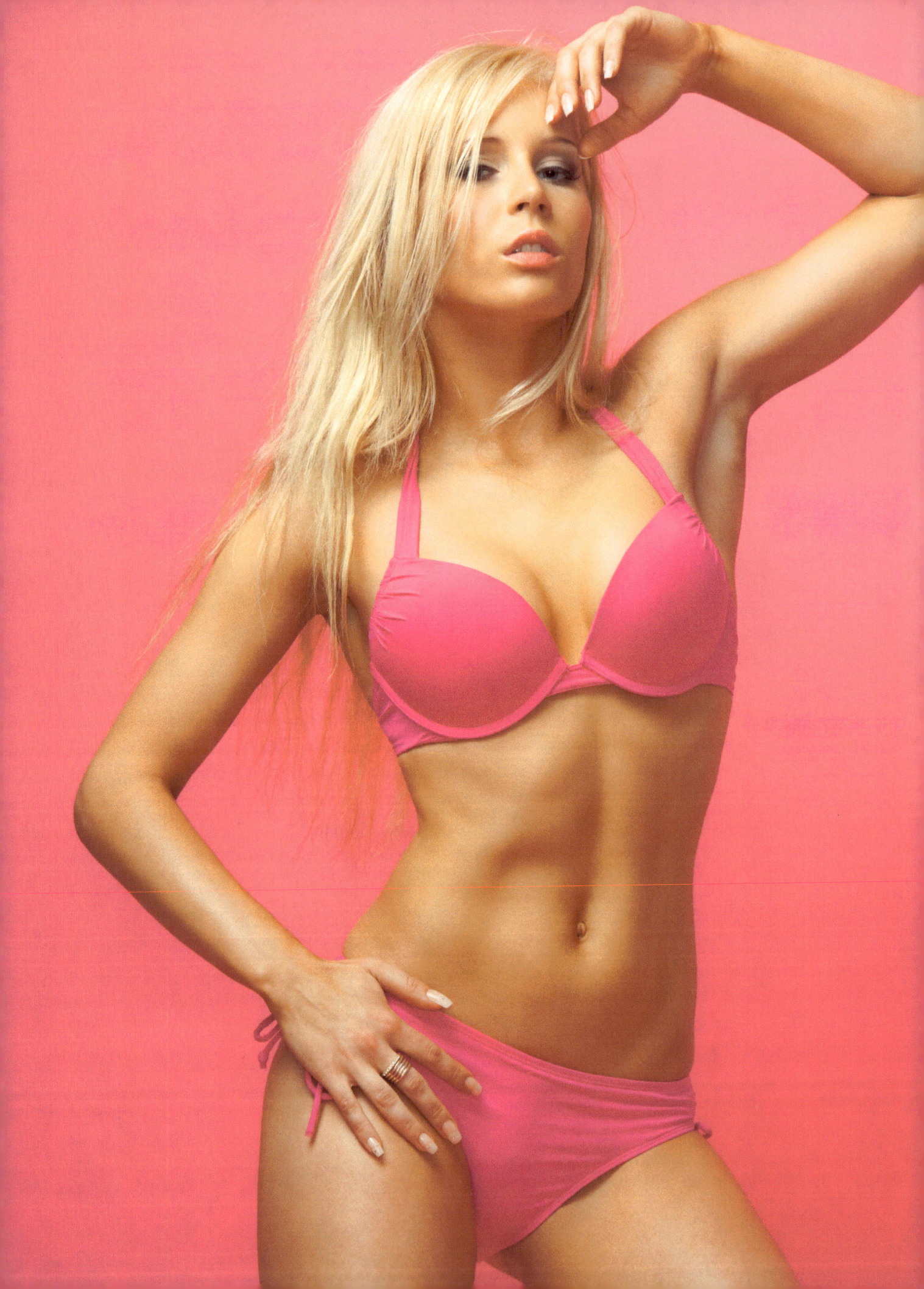

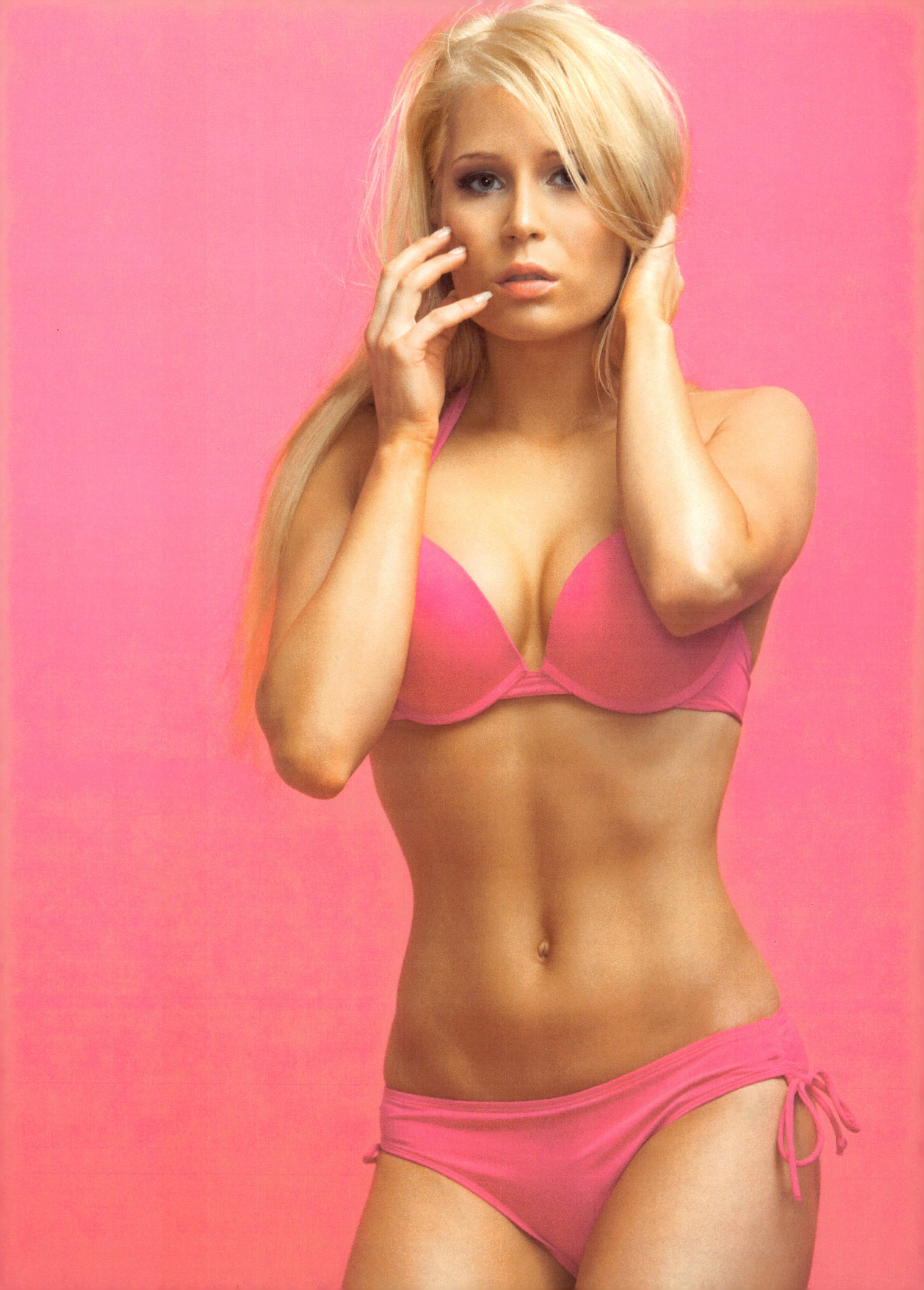

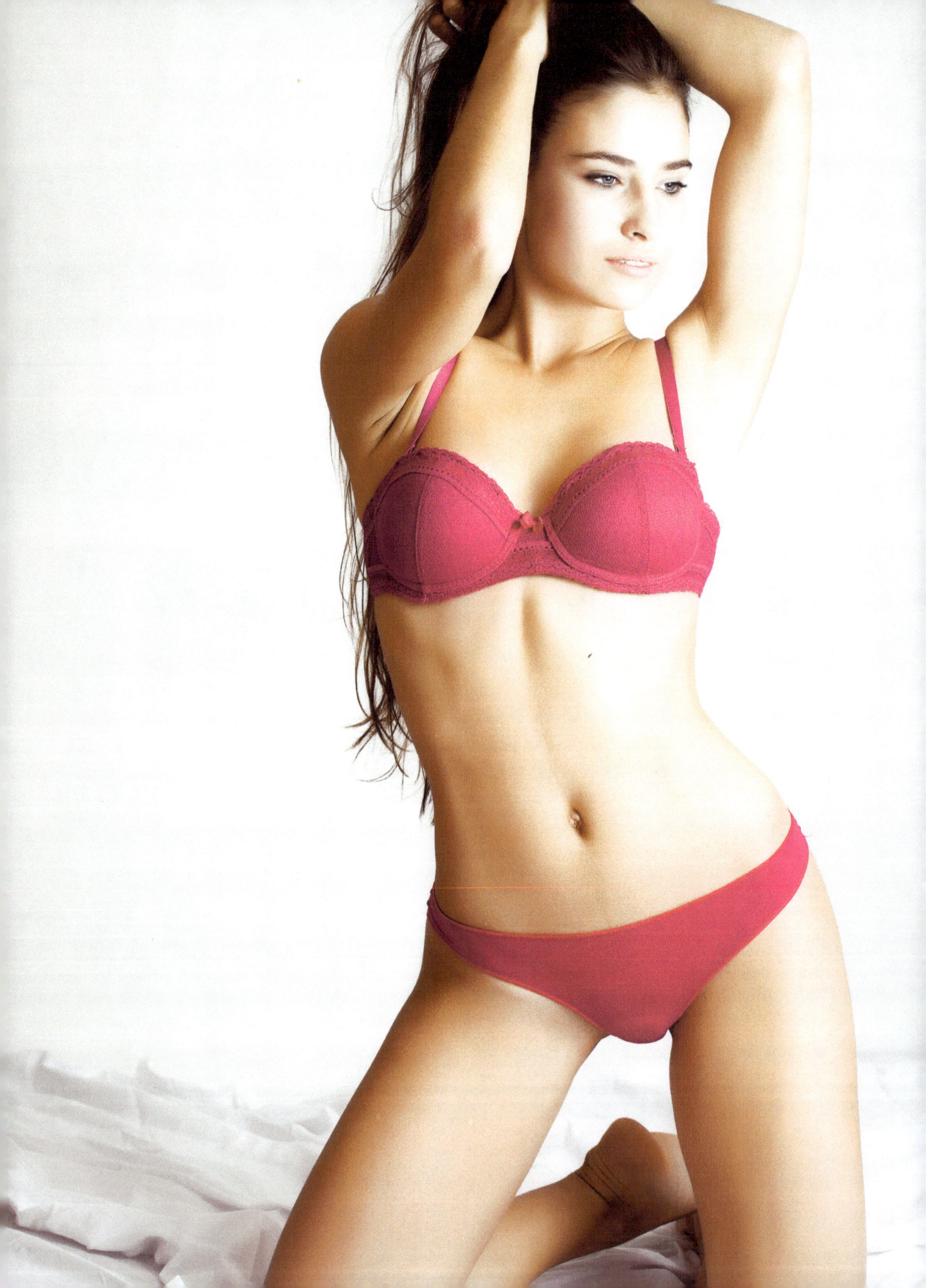

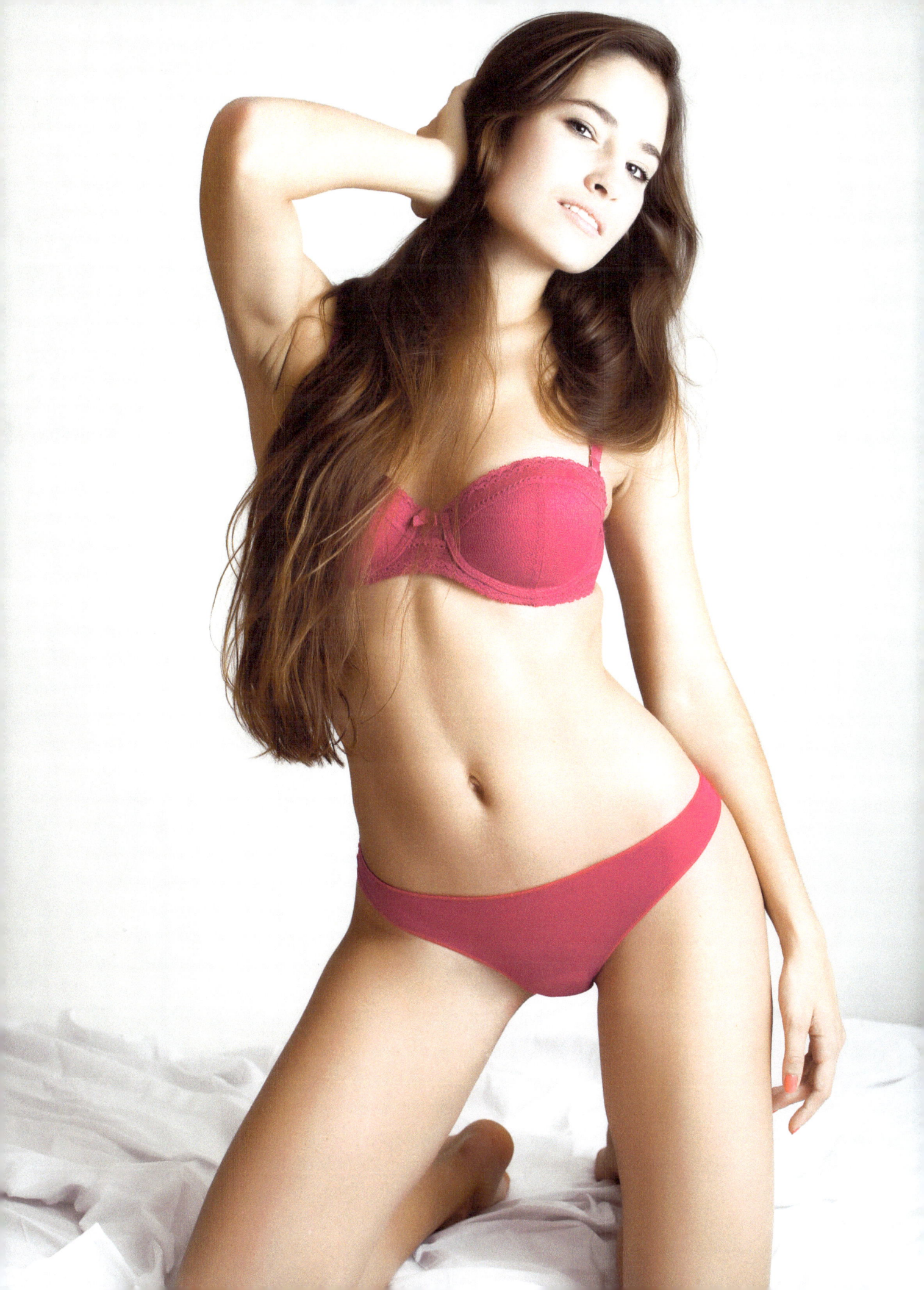

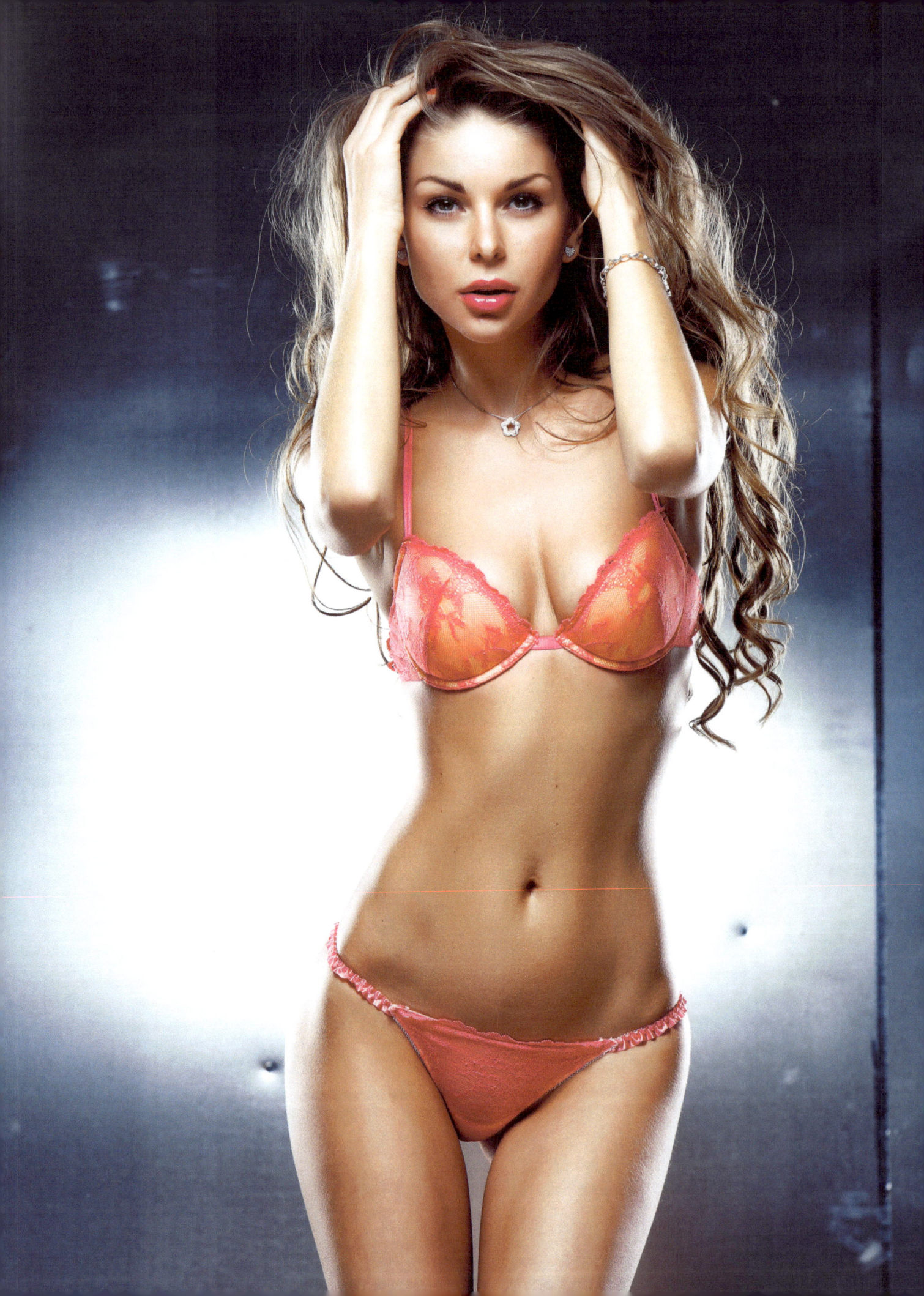

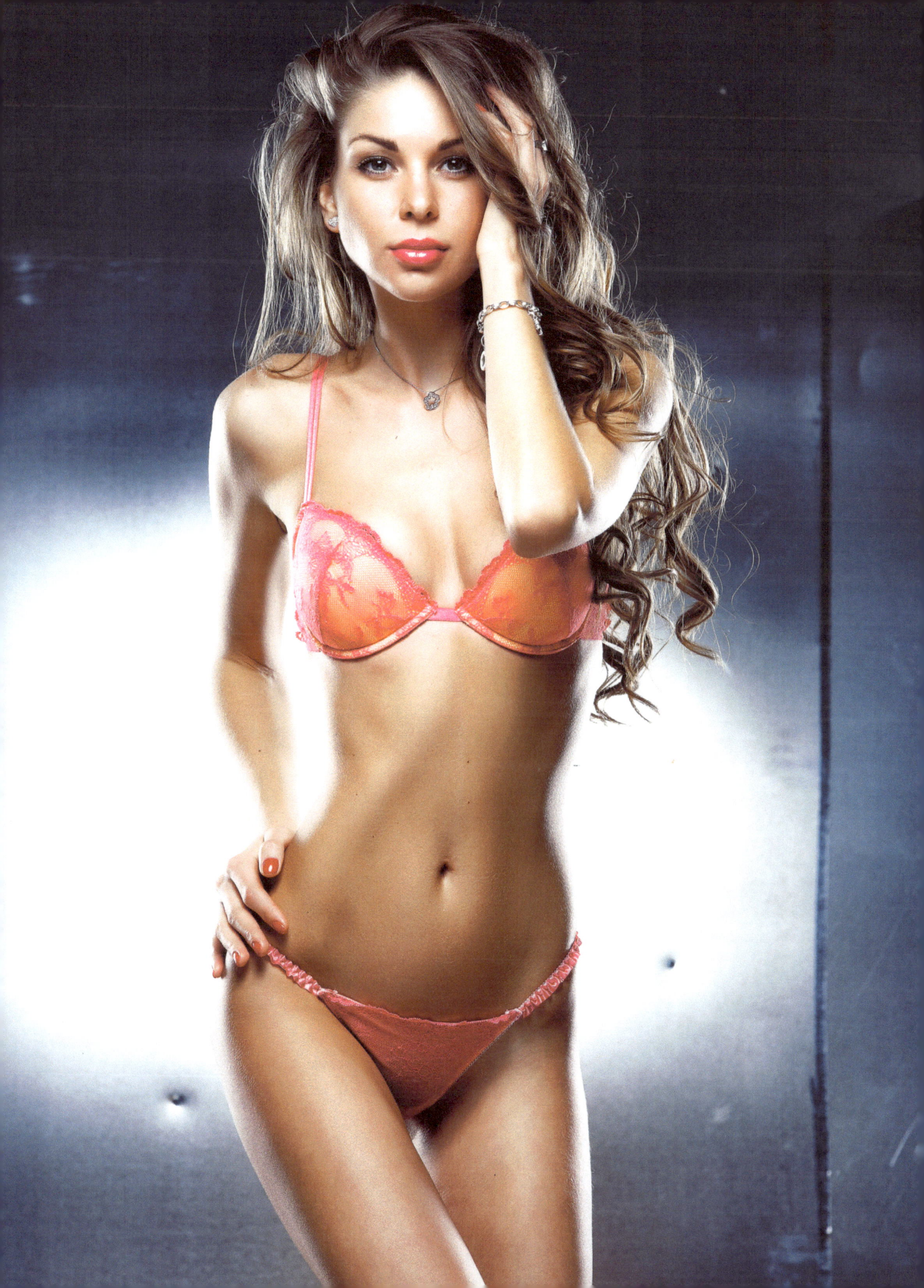

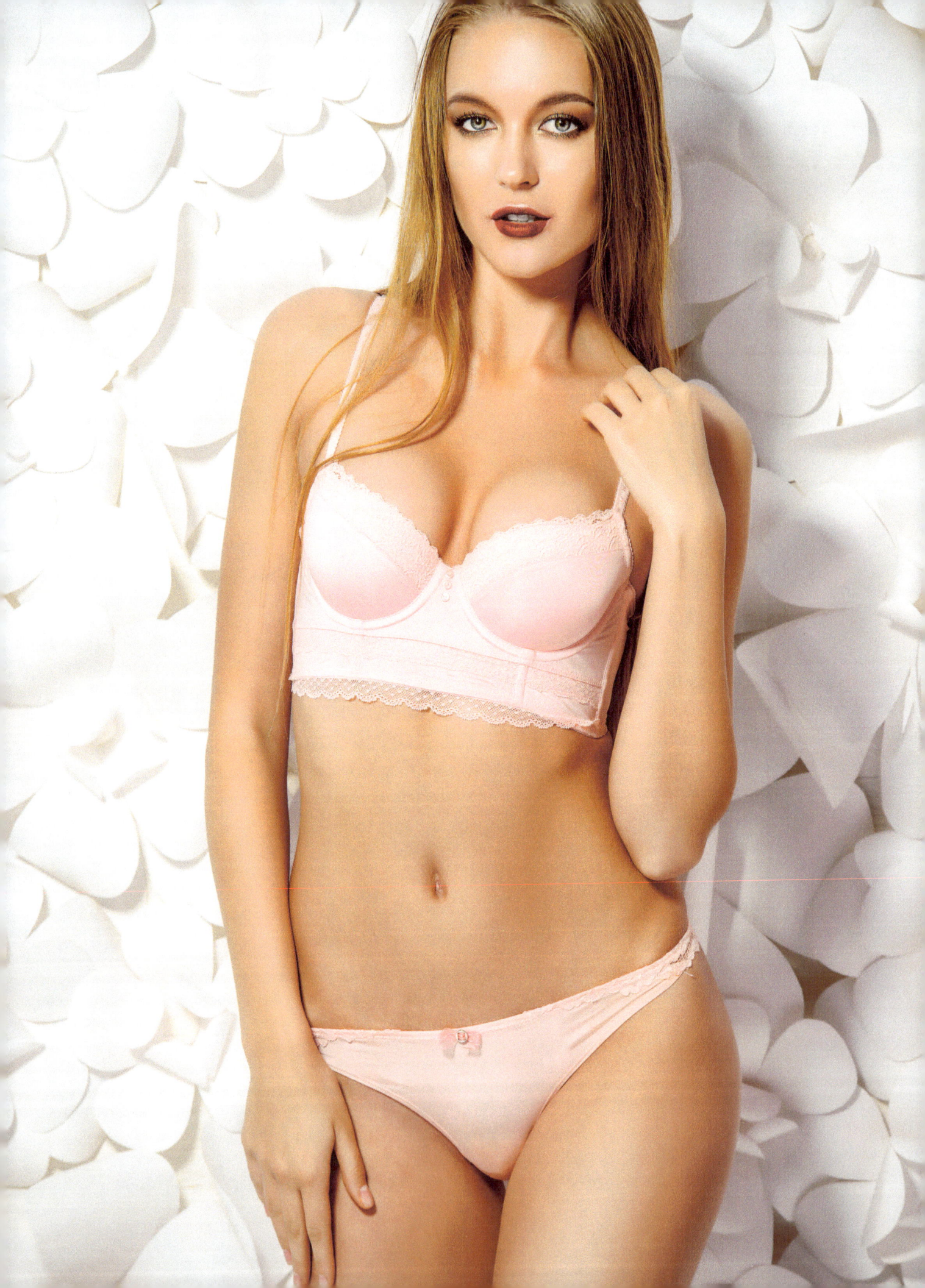

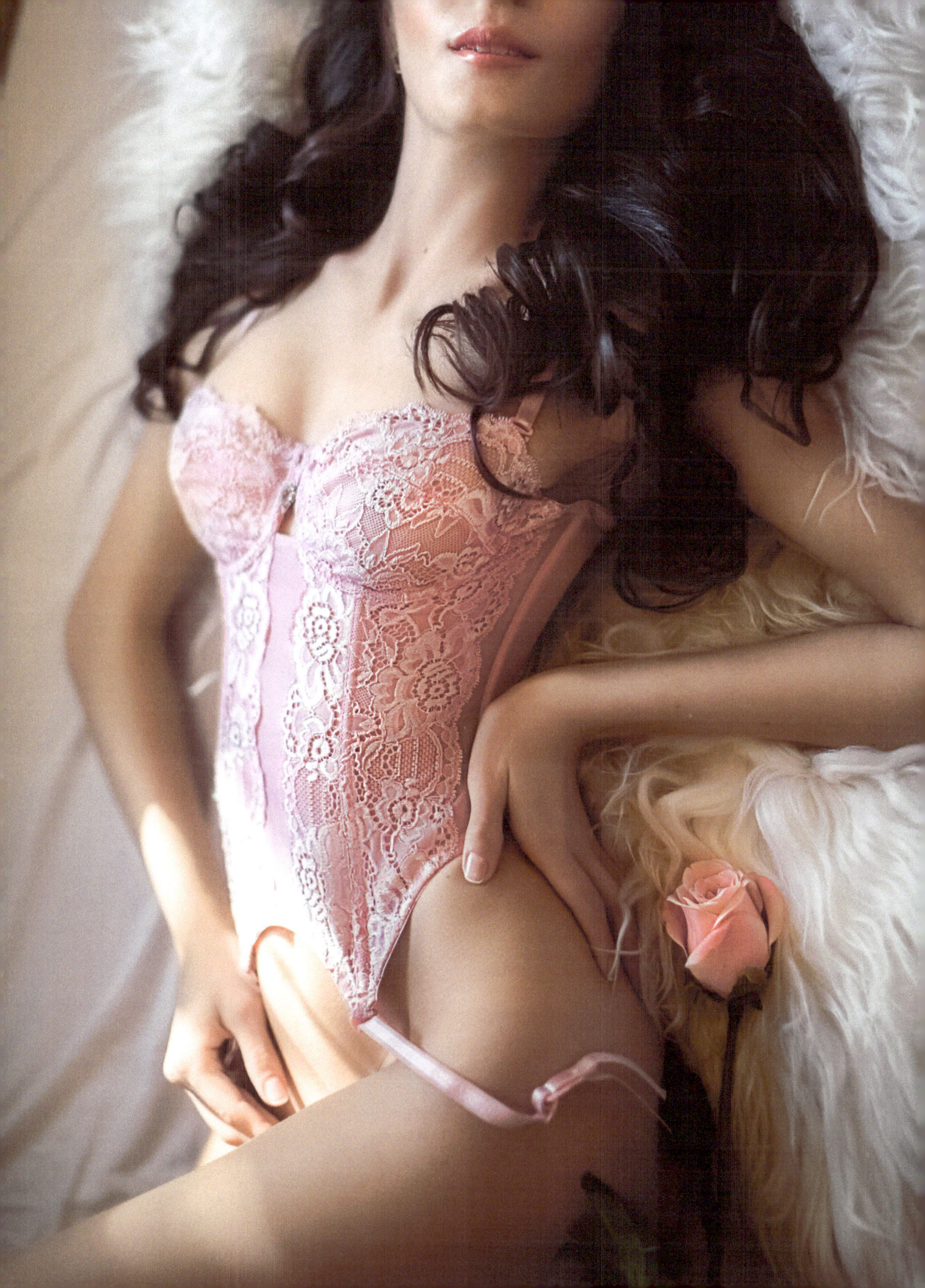

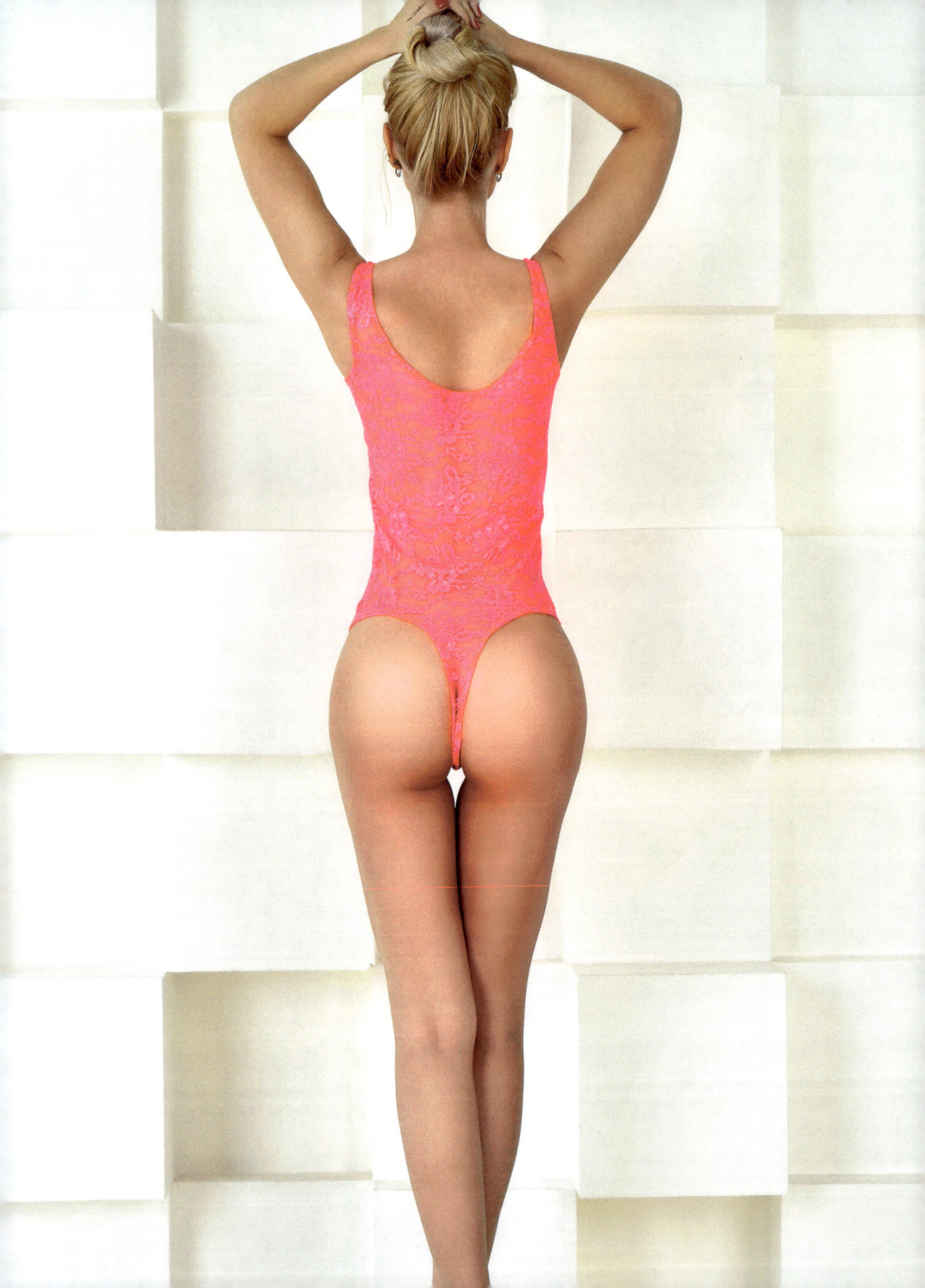

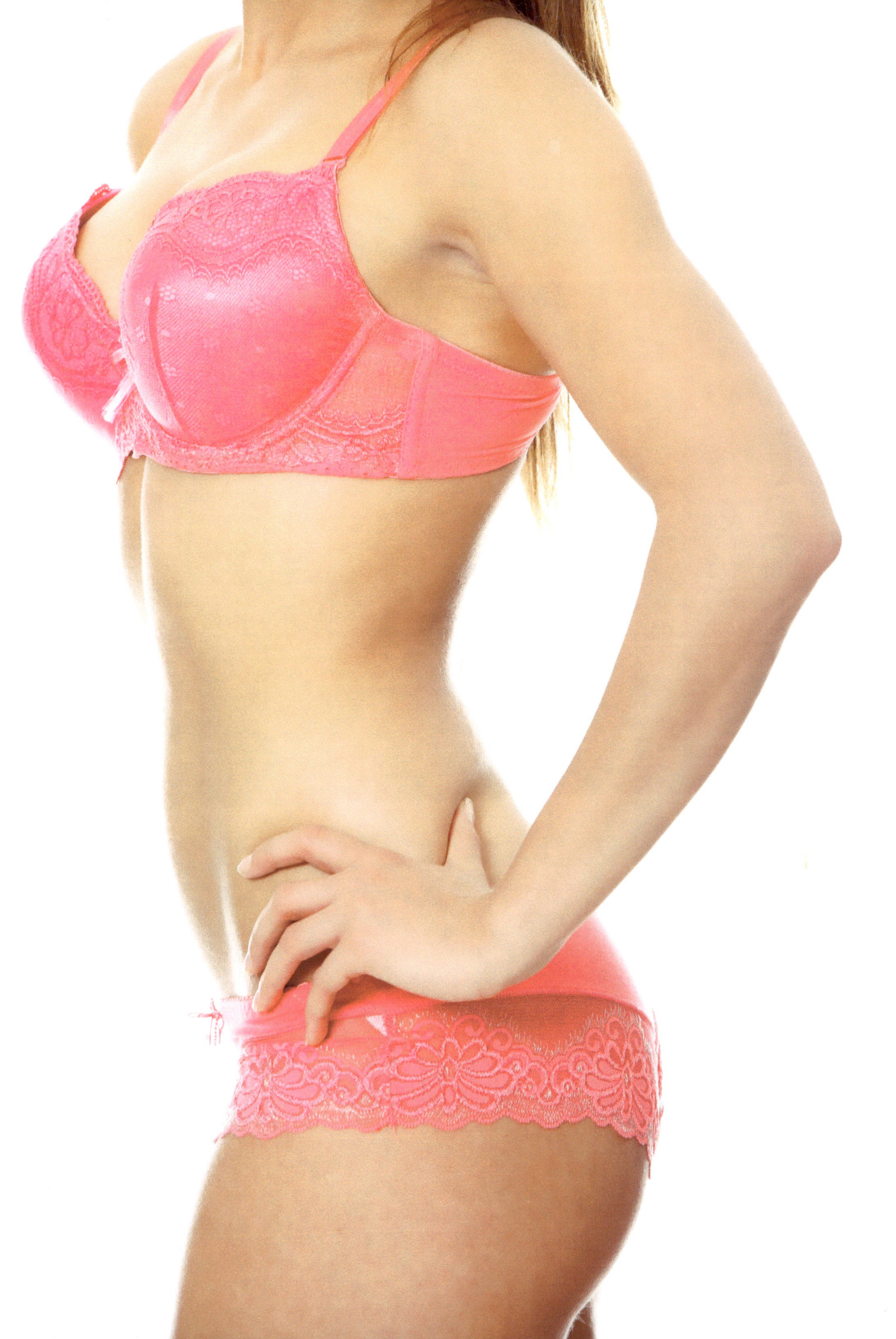

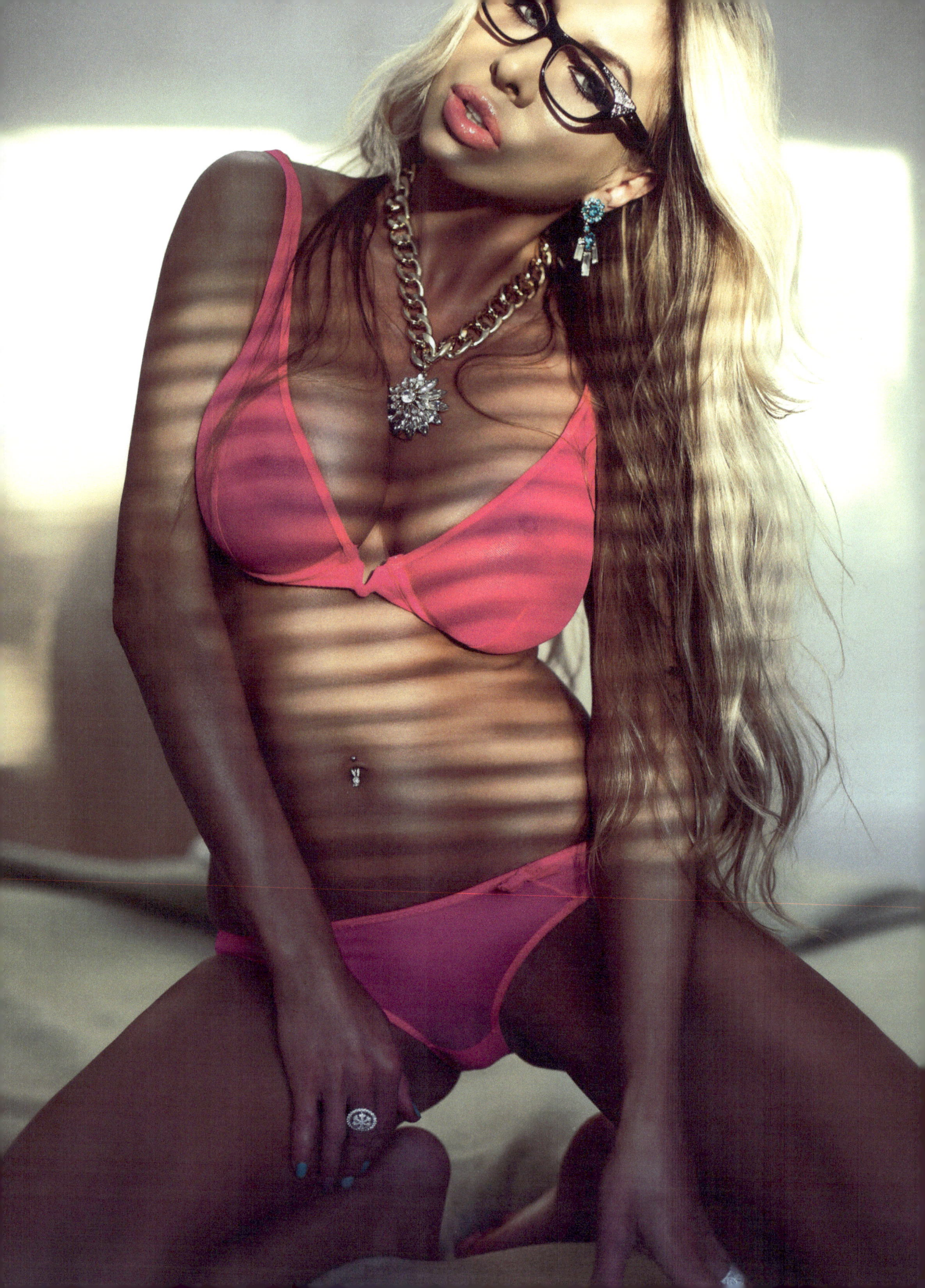

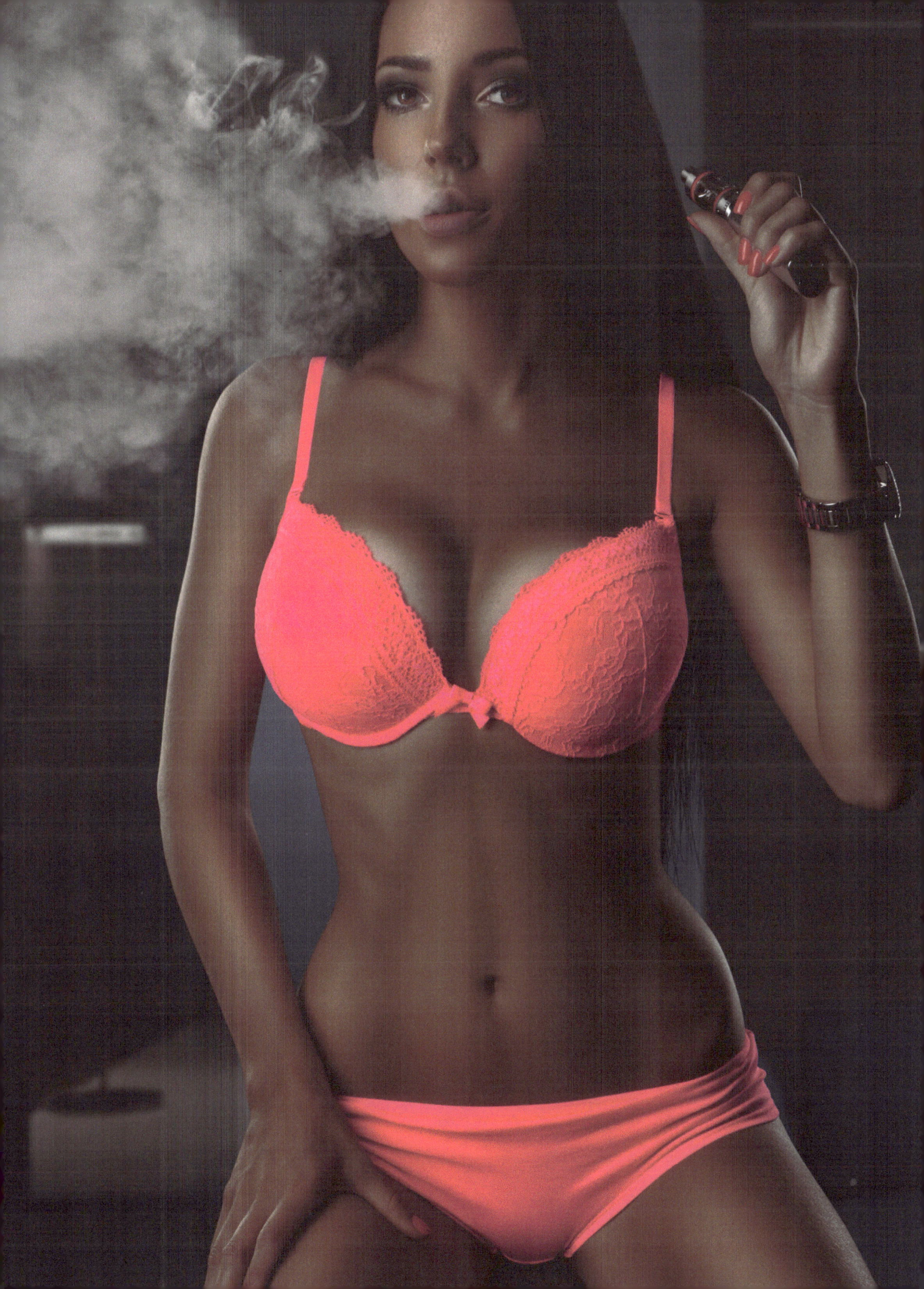

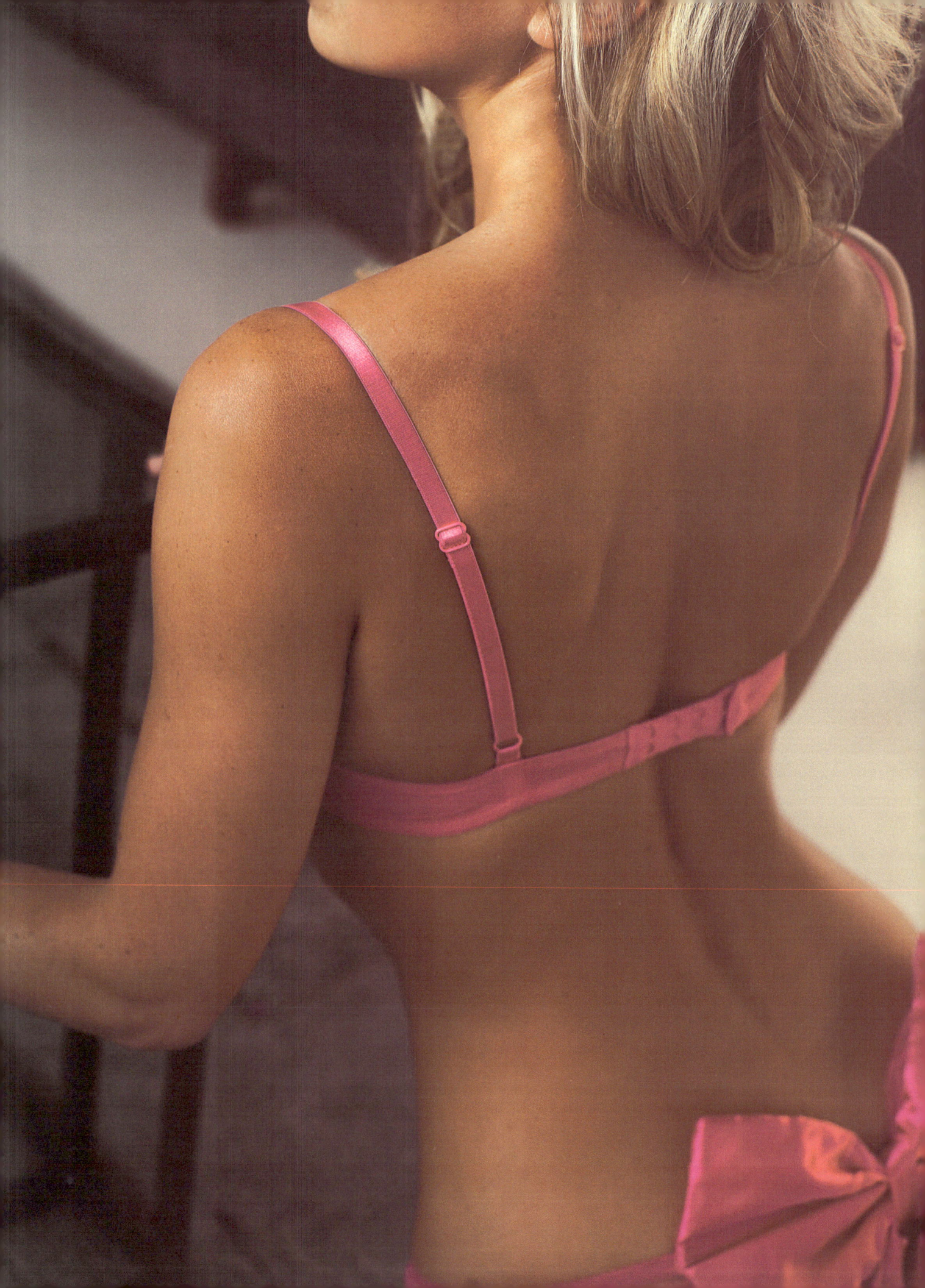

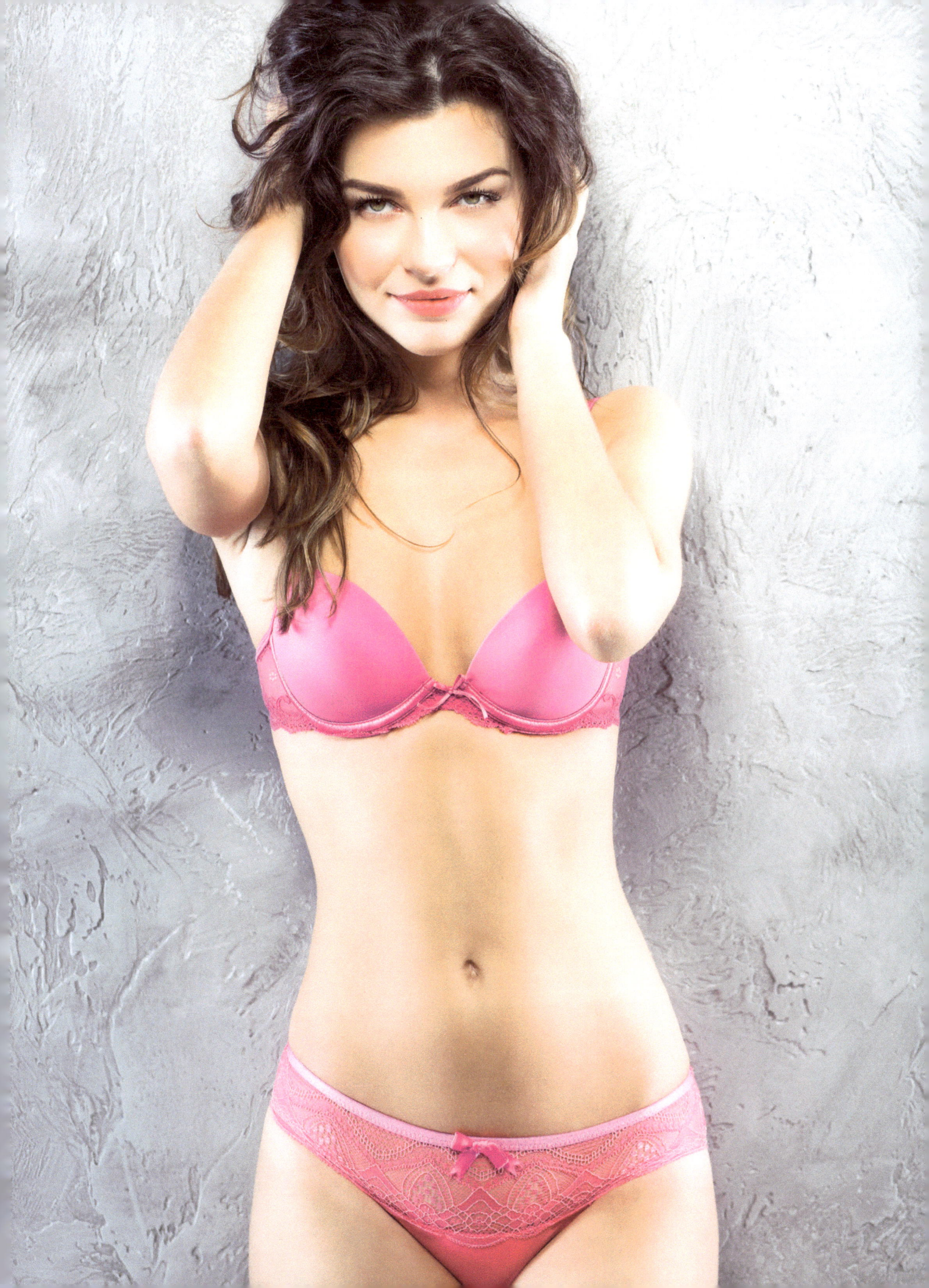

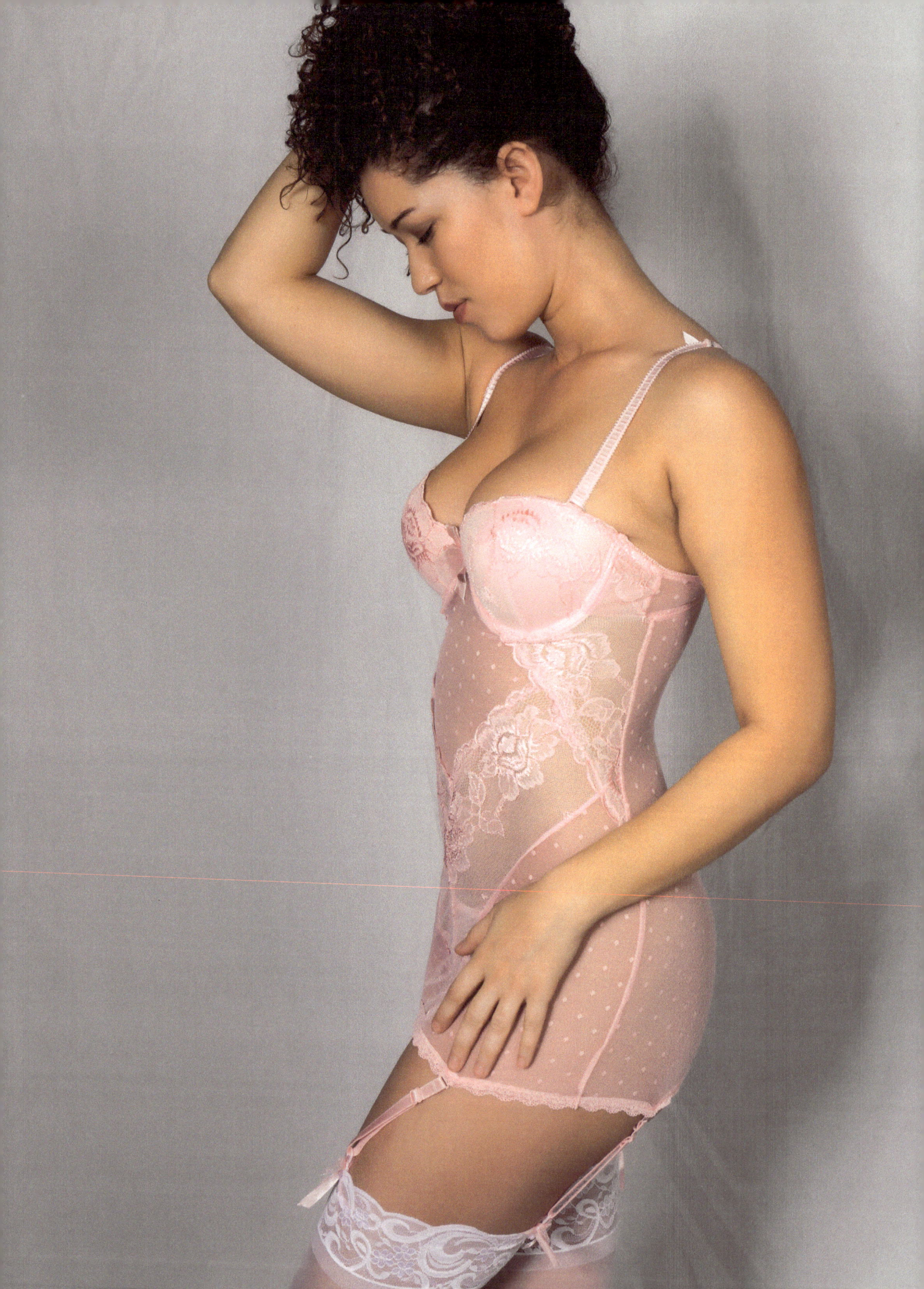

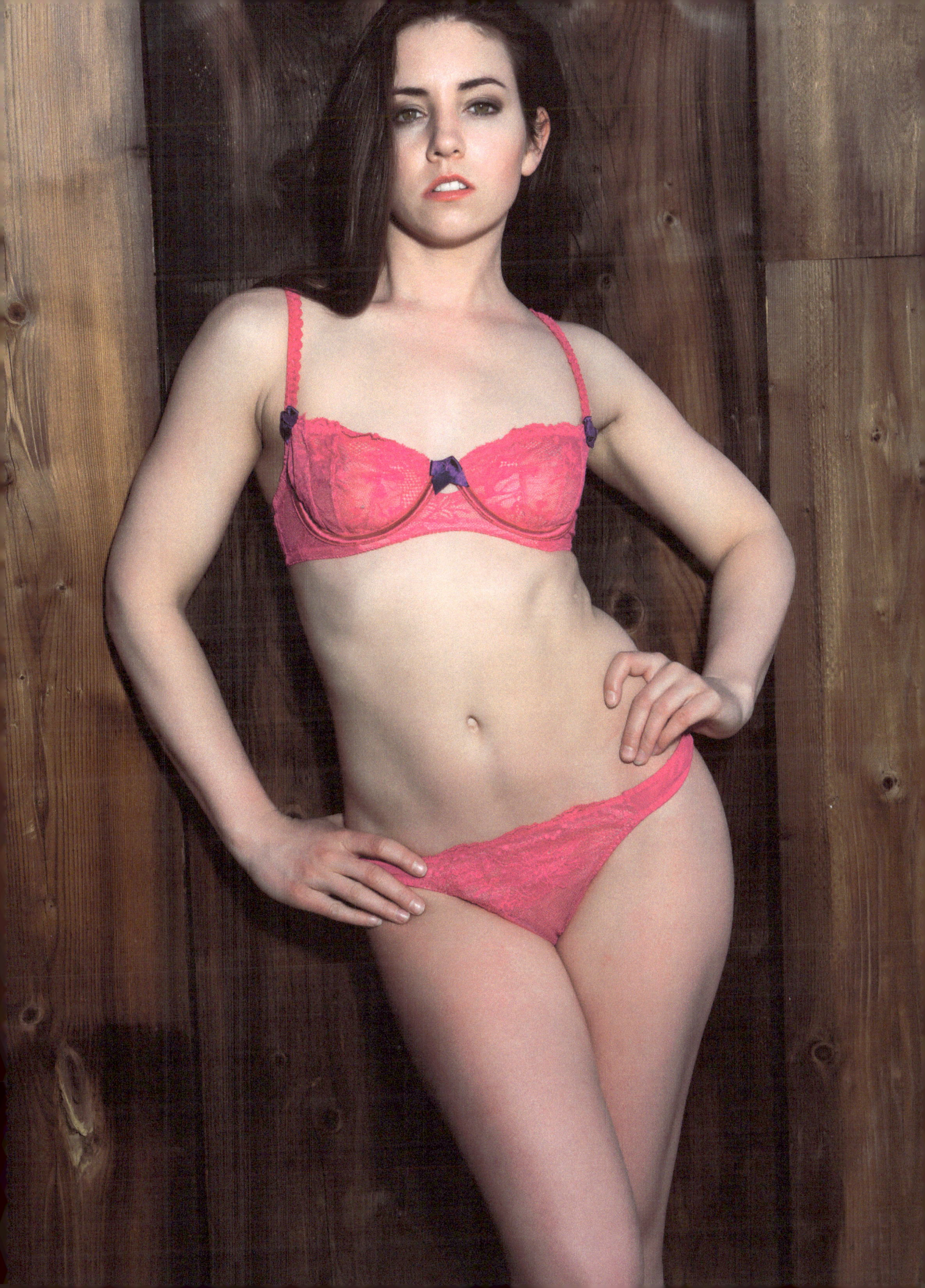

www.ingramcontent.com/pod-product-compliance
Lightning Source LLC
Chambersburg PA
CBHW050418180526
45159CB00005B/2316